FEB 3 - 2016
Grds 3-5

D1505992

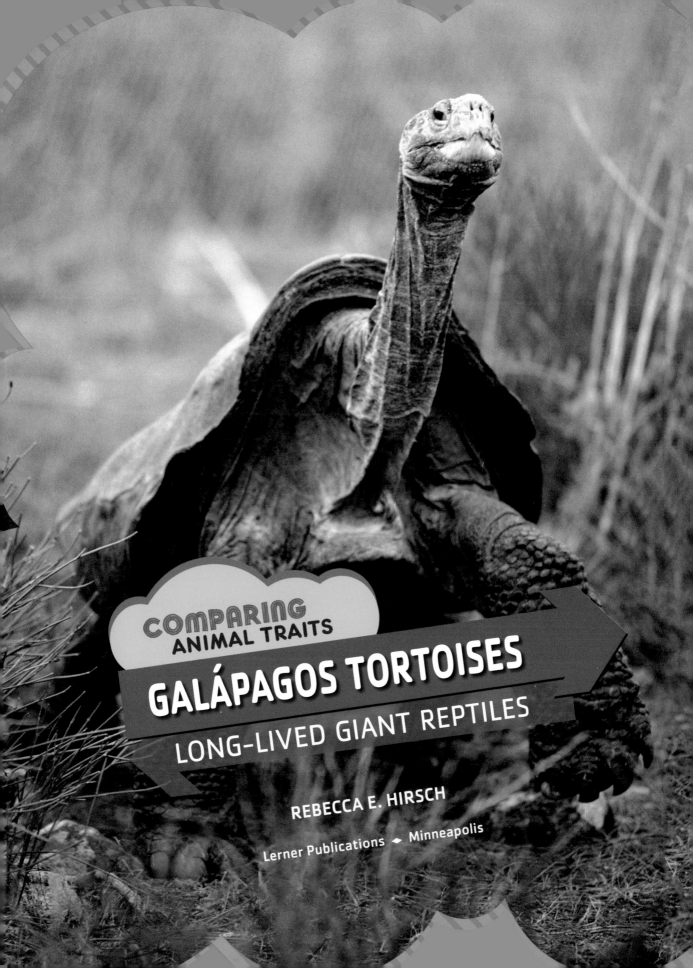

COMPARING ANIMAL TRAITS

GALÁPAGOS TORTOISES

LONG-LIVED GIANT REPTILES

REBECCA E. HIRSCH

Lerner Publications ◆ Minneapolis

Lerner Publications Company
A division of Lerner Publishing Group, Inc.
241 First Avenue North
Minneapolis, MN 55401 USA

For reading levels and more information, look up this title at www.lernerbooks.com.

Photo Acknowledgments

The images in this book are used with the permission of: © Tui De Roy/Minden Pictures/Getty Images, pp. 1, 4; Pete Oxford/Danita Delimont Photography/Newscom, p. 5; © iStockphoto.com/earleliason, p. 6; © Pablo Hidalgo/Fotos593/Shutterstock.com, pp. 7 (top), 18; © iStockphoto.com/Nancy Nehring, p. 7 (bottom left); Tui De Roy/Minden Pictures/Newscom, pp. 7 (bottom right), 19, 29 (left); © Danita Delimont/ Gallo Images/Getty Images, p. 8; © EBFoto/Shutterstock.com, p. 9 (left); © Thomas Roche/Moment Open/ Getty Images, p. 9 (right); © iStockphoto.com/CathyKeifer, p. 10; © Jarry/Shutterstock.com, p. 11 (top); © David Brabiner/Alamy, p. 11 (bottom); © Laura Westlund/Independent Picture Service, p. 12; © Prisma Bildagentur AG /Alamy, p. 13 (all); © Arco Images GmbH/Alamy, p. 14; © Chris Mattison/Alamy, p. 15 (top); © blickwinkel/Alamy, p. 15 (bottom); © Papilio/Alamy, p. 16; © Tony Bowler/Shutterstock.com, p. 20; © Timothy Craig Lubcke/Shutterstock.com, p. 21 (bottom); A.N.T. Photo Library/NHPA/Photoshot/Newscom, p. 21 (top); © Matt Jeppson/Shutterstock.com, p. 22; © Judy Bellah/Alamy, p. 23 (left); © John Mitchell/ Science Source/Getty Images, p. 23 (right); © Pete Oxford/naturepl.com, p. 24; Pete Oxford/Minden Pictures/ Newscom, p. 25 (top); © Rodrigo Buenia/AFP/Getty Images, p. 25 (bottom); © Ryan M. Bolton/Shutterstock. com, p. 26; © Larry Michael/naturepl.com, p. 27; © David A. Northcott/CORBIS, p. 28; © NHPA/SuperStock, p. 29 (right).

Front cover: © Millard H. Sharp/Getty Images.
Back cover: © iStockphoto.com/photoBlueIce.

Main body text set in Calvert MT Std 12/18. Typeface provided by Monotype Typography.

Library of Congress Cataloging-in-Publication Data

Hirsch, Rebecca E.
    Galápagos tortoises : long-lived giant reptiles / Rebecca E. Hirsch.
        pages cm. — (Comparing animal traits)
    Includes bibliographical references.
    Audience: Ages 7 to 10.
    Audience: Grades K to grade 3.
    ISBN 978-1-4677-7982-1 (lb : alk. paper) — ISBN 978-1-4677-8278-4 (pb : alk. paper) —
ISBN 978-1-4677-8279-1 (eb pdf)
    1. Galapagos tortoise—Juvenile literature. I. Title.
    QL666.C584H57 2015
    597.92'46—dc23   2015001957

Manufactured in the United States of America
1 – BP – 7/15/15

TABLE OF CONTENTS

Introduction
LET'S MEET THE GALÁPAGOS TORTOISE 4

Chapter 1
WHAT DO GALÁPAGOS TORTOISES LOOK LIKE? ...6

Chapter 2
WHERE DO GALÁPAGOS TORTOISES LIVE? 12

Chapter 3
THE SLOW, STEADY LIVES OF GALÁPAGOS TORTOISES 18

Chapter 4
THE LIFE CYCLE OF GALÁPAGOS TORTOISES 24

Galápagos Tortoise Trait Chart   30
Glossary   31
Selected Bibliography   32
Further Information   32
Index   32

LET'S MEET THE GALÁPAGOS TORTOISE

In a hole in the warm sand, a female Galápagos tortoise lays a dozen eggs. Three months later, baby tortoises crawl out of the hole. Each tortoise is tiny, about the size of a cookie. Someday they will grow up to be enormous. Galápagos tortoises belong to a group of animals called reptiles. Other animal groups you may know are insects, fish, amphibians, birds, and mammals.

A baby tortoise crawls out of its sandy nest.

All reptiles share certain traits. They are all vertebrates, animals with backbones. They have scaly skin on their bodies. And they are cold-blooded. That means they use their surroundings to warm and cool their bodies. While Galápagos tortoises have all these traits, they also have traits that make them different from other reptiles.

Galápagos tortoises are enormous reptiles.

CHAPTER 1

WHAT DO GALÁPAGOS TORTOISES LOOK LIKE?

Galápagos tortoises are huge reptiles. Adult males usually weigh 600 to 700 pounds (272 to 317 kilograms). Some can weigh a whopping 850 pounds (386 kg)! Female Galápagos tortoises are smaller and weigh 300 to 400 pounds (136 to 181 kg).

A Galápagos tortoise has thick, sturdy legs to support its weight. It has five claws on its front feet and four on its back feet. A Galápagos tortoise has a long neck and a beak-shaped jaw with no teeth. Tough, scaly skin protects its legs and head.

A Galápagos tortoise has claws on its feet for digging.

The dome tortoise (*left*) is larger than the saddleback tortoise (*right*).

The shell of a Galápagos tortoise can be more than 5 feet (1.5 meters) long and between 4 feet (1.2 m) and 5 feet across. The shell is made of two parts. The top shell is called the carapace. The shell under the tortoise's belly is called the plastron.

There are two types of Galápagos tortoises. They can be found on different islands. The largest tortoises are called domes. They have a high, round carapace. Other tortoises are smaller, with long necks, long legs, and carapaces that curve high above the neck, like a saddle. They are called saddlebacks. Each kind of tortoise is suited for survival in its own habitat.

DID YOU KNOW?
The shells of Galápagos tortoises are not solid. Inside, the carapace looks like a honeycomb with small pockets of air. This makes the shells LIGHTWEIGHT and easy to carry.

GALÁPAGOS TORTOISES VS. DESERT TORTOISES

A desert tortoise walks across the dry, rocky ground. Step by step, the tortoise slowly works its way through the desert. Desert tortoises inhabit dry parts of western North America. They reach 8.5 to 14 inches (22 to 36 centimeters) long and weigh between 8 and 15 pounds (3.6 to 6.8 kg). Although desert tortoises are much smaller than Galápagos tortoises, the two reptiles look a lot alike.

Both Galápagos tortoises and desert tortoises have thick legs and stubby feet with claws. Their scaly skin is gray or brown. Like Galápagos tortoises, desert tortoises have toothless, beak-shaped jaws.

A desert tortoise has a high, rounded shell, similar to domed Galápagos tortoises. The desert tortoise's shell is gray or brown and can have yellow or orange markings. As with the Galápagos tortoise, a desert tortoise has openings in its shell. The desert tortoise can pull its head and legs inside when danger is near.

COMPARE IT!

GALÁPAGOS TORTOISES

VS.

DESERT TORTOISES

300 TO 850 POUNDS
(136 TO 386 KG)

◄ BODY WEIGHT ►

8 TO 15 POUNDS
(3.6 TO 6.8 KG)

THICK LEGS WITH CLAWED FEET

◄ LIMBS ►

THICK LEGS WITH CLAWED FEET

◄ JAWS ►

Beak-shaped, no teeth

Beak-shaped, no teeth

GALÁPAGOS TORTOISES VS. VEILED CHAMELEONS

A veiled chameleon moves slowly along a green twig. With each step, its feet grip the branch tightly. Veiled chameleons live in the mountains of Yemen and Saudi Arabia in western Asia. Their body length can reach between 10 and 24 inches (25 and 61 cm) from the head to the tip of the tail. These small reptiles look very different from Galápagos tortoises. Instead of gray or brown skin, veiled chameleons have brightly colored scales. They may be blue, yellow, orange, green, or black, with bands of bright gold, yellow, orange, black, or tan. Unlike Galápagos tortoises, chameleons can change the color of their skin. Chameleons usually change color when they are scared or are protecting their homes.

Veiled chameleons can change the color of their skin.

A veiled chameleon's body is shaped differently than a Galápagos tortoise's body. A Galápagos tortoise is protected by a thick, bony shell. But a veiled chameleon has no shell. Its body is thin like a leaf. This slender shape helps the chameleon balance on narrow branches. A Galápagos tortoise has stocky legs and club-shaped feet. A veiled chameleon has slender legs and mitten-shaped feet for gripping branches.

DID YOU KNOW?

A veiled chameleon has a large helmetlike structure on its head called a **CASQUE**. The casque helps the chameleon drink. At night, droplets of dew collect on the casque and roll into the chameleon's mouth.

CHAPTER 2

WHERE DO GALÁPAGOS TORTOISES LIVE?

Galápagos tortoises live in the Galápagos, a group of volcanic islands off the western coast of South America. The islands have different types of Galápagos tortoises that are adapted for the islands' different habitats.

Saddlebacks live on hot, dry islands where tall cactuses and shrubs grow. Their long necks, long legs, and saddleback shells allow them to reach high and eat tall plants. Domes live on wetter islands with plenty of low-growing plants. They do not need to reach high for food, so their legs and necks are not as long.

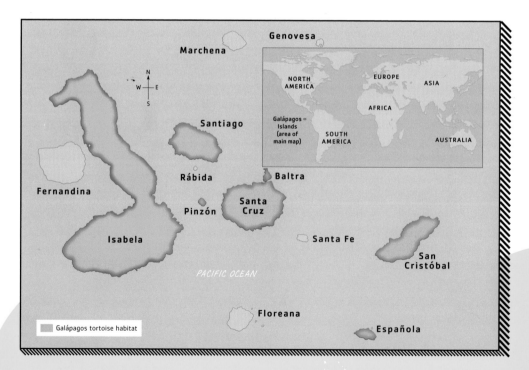

Galápagos tortoises travel through their habitat along well-worn paths. They graze on cactuses, grasses, leaves, flowers, and fruit. Galápagos tortoises bask in the sun. They are cold-blooded and use the sun's energy to warm their bulky bodies. When they need to cool down, they rest in muddy puddles, shallow ponds, or thick brush.

Some Galápagos tortoises migrate. During the dry season, they stay in high mountain meadows. In the rainy season, they travel downhill to feed in cool, grassy plains along the coast.

Galápagos tortoises are herbivores, or plant-eating animals.

GALÁPAGOS TORTOISES VS. LILFORD'S WALL LIZARDS

A Lilford's wall lizard rests on the rocky ground. A fly buzzes by, and the lizard catches the insect in its jaws. Lilford's wall lizards grow to about 2 to 3 inches (5 to 7.6 cm), not including their long tails. This lizard's habitat is similar to the habitat of Galápagos tortoises.

Both Galápagos tortoises and Lilford's wall lizards live on islands. Lilford's wall lizards live in the rocky Balearic Islands, off the coast of Spain. Some of the islands have forests, and others have only grasses. Lilford's wall lizards forage among the plants, looking for insects and fruit to eat.

A Lilford's wall lizard rests on a rock.

Lilford's wall lizards, like Galápagos tortoises, look different based on where they live. However, wall lizards don't have different shells or necks of different lengths. Instead, they are different colors. On some islands, wall lizards are a solid brown or greenish brown. In other places, their skin may have dark or light spots or they may have tails that are green, blue green, brown, or black. As with Galápagos tortoises, the different traits help wall lizards survive on each island's habitat. The colors may camouflage the lizards or help them find food.

DID YOU KNOW?
Lilford's wall lizards often rest on a flower called the dead horse arum lily. These flowers smell like **ROTTING MEAT.** The smell attracts flies and helps the lizards grab an easy meal.

15

GALÁPAGOS TORTOISES VS. OLIVE RIDLEY TURTLES

An olive ridley turtle glides through the blue ocean. It lifts its head above the water and takes a breath. Olive ridley turtles live in different habitats than Galápagos tortoises. Galápagos tortoises live on land. Olive ridley turtles swim in oceans.

While Galápagos tortoises live only in the Galápagos Islands, olive ridley turtles live around the world. They swim far from shore in tropical waters of the South Atlantic, Pacific, and Indian Oceans. They dive deep, up to 500 feet (152 m), looking for algae, shrimp, lobsters, crabs, fish, and mollusks to eat. They also sometimes hunt near shore.

Galápagos tortoises spend their entire lives on one island, moving along familiar paths. But olive ridley turtles wander

An olive ridley turtle swims through multiple oceans in its lifetime.

COMPARE IT!

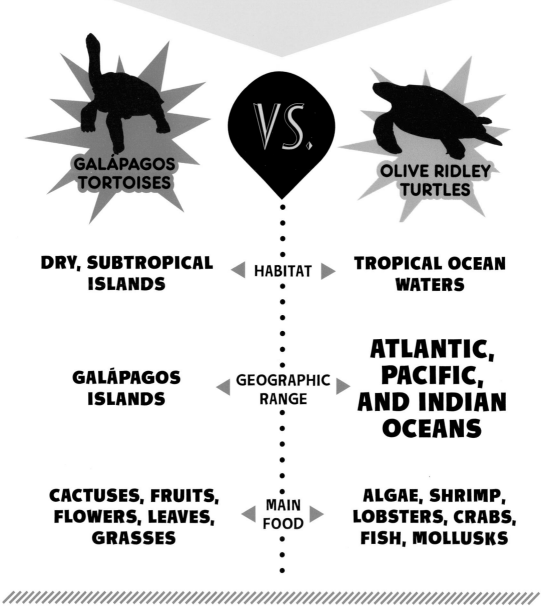

GALÁPAGOS TORTOISES **VS.** OLIVE RIDLEY TURTLES

GALÁPAGOS TORTOISES		OLIVE RIDLEY TURTLES
DRY, SUBTROPICAL ISLANDS	◄ HABITAT ►	TROPICAL OCEAN WATERS
GALÁPAGOS ISLANDS	◄ GEOGRAPHIC RANGE ►	ATLANTIC, PACIFIC, AND INDIAN OCEANS
CACTUSES, FRUITS, FLOWERS, LEAVES, GRASSES	◄ MAIN FOOD ►	ALGAE, SHRIMP, LOBSTERS, CRABS, FISH, MOLLUSKS

the wide ocean. Young turtles float on ocean currents and eat plankton. Adults swim and hunt larger creatures in the open ocean. Every few years, adult turtles migrate huge distances. They gather to mate near nesting beaches. Females then leave the water, crawling onto the sand to lay their eggs.

CHAPTER 3

THE SLOW, STEADY LIVES OF GALÁPAGOS TORTOISES

Galápagos tortoises lead relaxed lives. They rise in the morning and bask for an hour or two. Then they graze all morning. At midday, they rest in the shade to keep cool. In the afternoon, they graze again. By late afternoon, the tortoises are ready to sleep. Galápagos tortoises spend nearly sixteen hours a day snoozing.

Galápagos tortoises are very regular in their habits. They wake and sleep at the same time every day. They travel the same paths day after day. Their travel routes are so regular that their feet have carved paths into the ground.

DID YOU KNOW?
Each day, Galápagos tortoises walk only about **130 TO 160 FEET** (40 to 49 m). That's less than half the length of a football field.

Tortoises sometimes fight over mates or a good feeding spot. The tortoises face each other eye to eye, stand tall with mouths open, and stretch their necks high. The turtle that can stretch the tallest wins. The loser pulls his head in, lets out a noisy hissing sound, and retreats.

Two male Galápagos tortoises stretch their necks while fighting.

GALÁPAGOS TORTOISES VS. SHINGLEBACK LIZARDS

A shingleback lizard crawls across the open, sandy ground. Shingleback lizards inhabit dry forests and shrublands in Australia. These bulky lizards can be 12 to 14 inches (30 to 36 cm) long. Shingleback lizards have blue tongues. Their bumpy scales make them look like walking pinecones. These odd-looking lizards have behaviors similar to those of Galápagos tortoises.

Both Galápagos tortoises and shingleback lizards move slowly. Shingleback lizards creep steadily along the ground, looking for food to eat. They load up on plants and snack on slow-moving snails, slugs, and insects.

Shingleback lizards have distinctive blue tongues.

Snails are a main food source for shingleback lizards.

Shingleback lizards are active during the day and have a set routine, similar to Galápagos tortoises. In the morning, shingleback lizards bask in the sun to warm their bodies. As the day warms up, they search for food. When evening falls, they rest in bushes and dens of other animals underground. Like Galápagos tortoises, they usually stay in a small home area and don't travel far.

DID YOU KNOW?
The slow-moving shingleback lizard can't outrun most predators. Instead, it tries to **SCARE** them away. It waves its dark blue tongue, hisses, and widens its body to make it look bigger.

GALÁPAGOS TORTOISES VS. COPPERHEAD SNAKES

A copperhead snake lies quietly in the grass. When a mouse runs by, the snake strikes with a deadly bite. These reddish-brown snakes live in Mexico and the southeastern United States. They grow to about 30 inches (76 cm) long. Copperhead snakes have different behaviors than Galápagos tortoises.

Galápagos tortoises spend their days grazing on plants. But copperheads are predators. They eat mice, birds, lizards, snakes, insects, and other small animals. Galápagos tortoises move slowly, but copperhead snakes can strike with lightning speed. They wait for prey to come near and then kill with a bite from their deadly fangs, which are used to inject venom.

Galápagos tortoises have a set daily routine. But copperhead snakes do not. During the hot summer, a copperhead sleeps during the day and hunts at night. In spring and fall, the routine switches. The snake hunts during the day and sleeps at night. In winter, copperheads hibernate in dens in rocky hillsides.

Copperhead snakes wait for their prey to come near before they strike.

COMPARE IT!

GALÁPAGOS TORTOISES

VS.

COPPERHEAD SNAKES

GRASS, LEAVES, CACTUS

◀ WHAT IT EATS ▶

MICE, BIRDS, LIZARDS

◀ HOW IT GETS FOOD ▶

Grazes

Kills prey with a venomous bite

DAY

◀ WHEN IT IS ACTIVE ▶

DAY IN SPRING AND FALL, NIGHT IN SUMMER, HIBERNATES DURING THE WINTER

CHAPTER 4

THE LIFE CYCLE OF GALÁPAGOS TORTOISES

Galápagos tortoises mate between January and August.
After mating, female Galápagos tortoises walk to nesting areas
several miles away and dig holes in dry, sandy ground with
their hind feet. They lay two to twenty-five hard-shelled eggs the
size of baseballs. Next, they use their feet to cover the eggs with
sand. Then the females leave. Their work is done.

The temperature of the nest controls the sex of the tortoise
hatchlings. If the nest is warm, more females develop. If the
nest is cool, more males develop. After three to five months, the

A female Galápagos tortoise digs her nest.

young tortoises crawl out of their eggs. Each tortoise hatchling is about 2.5 inches (6.3 cm) long and weighs about 3 ounces (85 grams). The hatchlings are on their own right away. Without their mothers to help them, many will die young. Only a few will become adults. Galápagos tortoises reach adult size in 20 to 25 years. They can live a long time, between 100 and 150 years.

The sex of a Galápagos tortoise hatchling depends on the temperature of the nest.

DID YOU KNOW?

Lonesome George was the **ONLY** tortoise left on Pinta Island, one of the Galápagos Islands. People tried to help George mate, but their attempts failed. In 2012, Lonesome George died, leaving no more of his kind on the island.

GALÁPAGOS TORTOISES VS. BLANDING'S TURTLES

A Blanding's turtle rests along the weedy edge of a pond. Startled by a sound nearby, it dives into the water with a splash. Blanding's turtles are medium-sized turtles with shells 6 to 9 inches (15 to 23 cm) long. They live in shallow lakes, ponds, marshes, and swamps around the Great Lakes in North America. Blanding's turtles have a life cycle that is similar to that of Galápagos tortoises.

Like most reptiles, Galápagos tortoises and Blanding's turtles lay eggs. After mating, female Blanding's turtles travel to sandy areas to lay their eggs. Each female lays six to twenty-one eggs in a hole in the sand.

A Blanding's turtle's shell will grow to be 6 to 9 inches (15 to 23 cm) long.

As with Galápagos tortoises, nest temperature controls the number of males and females. Warm nests produce more females. Cool nests produce more males. In two months, the eggs hatch and the hatchlings crawl out of the ground.

Similar to Galápagos tortoises, Blanding's turtles grow slowly and live a long time. Blanding's turtles reach adulthood when they are 14 to 20 years old. They can live 70 years or more, compared to 100 to 150 years for Galápagos tortoises.

GALÁPAGOS TORTOISES VS. MONKEY-TAILED SKINKS

A young monkey-tailed skink clings to its mother's back. The youngster rides along as its mother climbs through the trees. Monkey-tailed skinks live in forests on the Solomon Islands near Papua New Guinea and Australia. They grow to about 28 inches (72 cm) from the head to the tip of the tail. These lizards have very different life cycles than Galápagos tortoises.

Unlike Galápagos tortoises, female monkey-tailed skinks give birth to live young. Six to eight months after mating, one or two babies are born. Each baby skink is almost half the size of its mother. Unlike a Galápagos tortoise, a young skink stays with its parents for about a year. The parents carry the youngster and protect it from predators.

Monkey-tailed skinks grow up faster than Galápagos tortoises. The skinks reach adulthood in about two years. They live shorter lives too. A monkey-tailed skink lives for only about fifteen years.

Unlike Galápagos tortoises, monkey-tailed skinks stay with their young for a year to help protect them.

COMPARE IT!

GALÁPAGOS TORTOISES

VS.

MONKEY-TAILED SKINKS

2 to 25 eggs

AVERAGE NUMBER OF ◄ YOUNG ► AT HATCHING/ BIRTH

1 to 2 live young

20 TO 25 YEARS

◄ AGE AT ADULTHOOD ►

2 YEARS

100 TO 150 YEARS

◄ TYPICAL LIFE SPAN ►

15 YEARS

GALÁPAGOS TORTOISE TRAIT CHART

This book introduces Galápagos tortoises and explores the ways they are similar to and different from other reptiles. What favorite reptiles would you add to this list?

	COLD-BLOODED	SCALES ON BODY	LAY EGGS	BONY SHELL	LIVES ON ISLANDS	EAT MOSTLY PLANTS
GALÁPAGOS TORTOISE	X	X	X	X	X	X
DESERT TORTOISE	X	X	X	X		X
VEILED CHAMELEON	X	X	X			
LILFORD'S WALL LIZARD	X	X	X		X	
OLIVE RIDLEY TURTLE	X	X	X	X		
SHINGLEBACK LIZARD	X	X				X
COPPERHEAD SNAKE	X	X				
BLANDING'S TURTLE	X	X	X	X		
MONKEY-TAILED SKINK	X	X			X	X

GLOSSARY

adapted: suited to living in a particular environment

bask: to lie or rest in warm air

camouflage: to hide or disguise an animal by covering it up or changing the way it looks

carapace: the upper shell of a turtle

dens: shelters or resting places for animals

habitat: an environment where an animal naturally lives. A habitat is the place where an animal can find food, water, air, shelter, and a place to raise its young.

hatchlings: recently hatched animals

hibernate: to become inactive during winter

migrate: to move from one place to another for feeding or breeding

mollusks: animals such as snails, clams, and octopuses with a soft body and usually enclosed in a hard shell

parasites: living things that live in or on other living things

plankton: the tiny floating or weakly swimming animal and plant life of a body of water

plastron: the lower shell of a turtle

predators: animals that hunt, or prey on, other animals

prey: an animal that is hunted and killed by a predator for food

traits: features that are inherited from parents. Body size and skin color are examples of inherited traits.

venom: poison produced by some animals like snakes and passed to a victim usually by biting or stinging

volcanic: produced by a volcano

LERNER

Expand learning beyond the printed book. Download free, complementary educational resources for this book from our website, www.lernerresource.com.

SOURCE

SELECTED BIBLIOGRAPHY

Franklin, Carl J. *Turtles: An Extraordinary Natural History 245 Million Years in the Making*. Saint Paul: Voyageur Press, 2007.

"Galapagos Tortoise, *Geochelone nigra*." San Diego Zoo. Accessed November 18, 2014. http://library.sandiegozoo.org/factsheets/galapagos_tortoise/tortoise.htm.

"Giant Tortoises." Galapagos Conservancy. Accessed November 10, 2014. http://www.galapagos.org/about_galapagos/tortoises/.

O'Shea, Mark, and Tim Halliday. *Reptiles and Amphibians*. New York: Dorling Kindersley, 2002.

FURTHER INFORMATION

Chin, Jason. *Island: A Story of the Galápagos*. New York: Roaring Brook, 2012. Discover the exciting history of the Galápagos Islands and how plants and animals came to live there.

Galapagos Conservancy—Sustainable Society: Giant Tortoise Webcam Project http://www.galapagos.org/conservation/galapagos-giant-tortoise-webcam-project Learn more about how scientists are working to save the Galápagos tortoise and watch tortoises on the live webcam.

George, Jean Craighead. *Galápagos George*. New York: HarperCollins, 2014. Read about Lonesome George, a Galápagos tortoise who was the last tortoise from Pinta Island.

San Diego Zoo Animals—Galápagos Tortoise http://animals.sandiegozoo.org/animals/galapagos-tortoise Explore Galápágos tortoise photos and facts.

Storad, Conrad J. *Galápagos Tortoises*. Minneapolis: Lerner Publications, 2009. Learn more about Galápagos tortoises and see vivid photographs.

INDEX

Asia, 10
Australia, 20, 28

Balearic Islands, 14
Blanding's turtles, 26–27

carapace, 7
copperhead snakes, 22–23

desert tortoises, 8–9
diet, 13, 14, 22
domes, 7, 12

Galápagos Islands, 12, 16

habitat, 7, 8, 10, 12, 13, 14–15, 16, 20, 21, 26

Indian Ocean, 16

life cycle, 24–25, 26, 27, 28
Lilford's wall lizards, 14–15

Mexico, 22
migration, 13, 17
monkey-tailed skinks, 28–29

North America, 8, 26

olive ridley turtles, 16–17

Pacific Ocean, 16
plastron, 7

reptiles, 4–5, 6, 8, 10, 26

saddlebacks, 7, 12
shingleback lizards, 20–21
Solomon Islands, 28
South Atlantic Ocean, 16

trait chart, 30

United States, 22

veiled chameleons, 10–11